Rita Mulcahy's™

Hot Topics

Flashcards for Passing the PMP® and CAPM® Exams

Sixth Edition

Rita Mulcahy, PMP

Second Printing

ISBN 978-1-932735-22-2
Library of Congress Control Number
2009923724
Printed in the U.S.A.

E-mail: info@rmcproject.com
Web: www.rmcproject.com
Phone: 952.846.4484

WARNING: This is not a stand–alone product! You will need other review materials in order to pass the PMP or CAPM exam. We make no warranties or representations that use of these materials will result in passage of either exam. This book is designed to work with the book *PMP® Exam Prep, Sixth Edition*, and the book *CAPM® Exam Prep, Second Edition*. Both books are written by Rita Mulcahy, PMP, and are available at www.rmcproject.com. Use the chapter references on each Hot Topics flashcard to find further information in the PMP or CAPM Exam Prep Book.

TABLE OF CONTENTS

HOW TO USE THIS BOOK: This book has been updated for the *PMBOK® Guide, Fourth Edition*. It is a portable reference to the Hot Topics on the PMP and CAPM exams, to be used to improve test taking speed and information recall. Note that the Professional and Social Responsibility chapter is not covered in the CAPM exam.

Read the front of each page and see if you can recall the items on the back of the page and know what they mean. If studying for the PMP exam, review Hot Topics you are unfamiliar with in the book *PMP® Exam Prep, Sixth Edition* and the *PMBOK® Guide, Fourth Edition*. If you are studying for the CAPM exam, Hot Topics you are unfamiliar with should be reviewed in the book *CAPM® Exam Prep, Second Edition* and the *PMBOK® Guide, Fourth Edition*. An audio version of Hot Topics is also available on CD-ROM.

ABOUT US

▶ Rita Mulcahy, PMP, is an internationally recognized expert in project management and a highly sought-after project management author, trainer, and speaker.

RITA MULCAHY, PMP

She has over 30 best-selling project management resources to her credit, and has been a Contributor and Reviewer to the Project Management Body of Knowledge (*PMBOK® Guide*).

▶ Rita has taught and spoken to tens of thousands of managers and executives, and her products, classes, and e-Learning courses have helped over 250,000 people become more effective at managing projects.

► Rita is also the founder of RMC Project Management, an international project management speaking, training, and consulting firm, a Global Registered Education Provider with PMI, and one of the fastest-growing training companies in the country. RMC specializes in real-world project management training—interpreting the *PMBOK® Guide* for real-world use and helping companies use the latest project management tools and techniques to complete projects faster, with less expense, better results, and fewer resources.

See us at www.rmcproject.com

PMP EXAM PREP PRODUCTS

Rita Mulcahy's PMP® EXAM PREP, SIXTH EDITION
This is the only accelerated guide to the PMP exam, and is currently used in more than 40 countries.

This Course in a Book® contains review material, exercises, activities, games, and insider tips, and can decrease study time to only about 120 hours.

Rita Mulcahy's PM FASTRACK® EXAM SIMULATION SOFTWARE
PM FASTrack® is based on a psychometric review with more than 1,500 questions in six testing modes.

TAKE A COURSE

PROJECT MANAGEMENT TRICKS OF THE TRADE®
This three-day PM course covers the project management process using PMI terminology with real-world applications.

PMP® EXAM PREP COURSE
This two-day accelerated learning course is designed to help you prepare for the PMP exam with the most understanding of project management and the least amount of study! Study less than 40 hours after taking the course! This course includes the PMP® Exam Prep System.

See the rest of our PMP and CAPM exam prep products at www.rmcproject.com.

What is the definition of a project?

Temporary

Creates a unique product or service

What is the definition of a program?

A group of interrelated projects,
managed in a coordinated way

What is the definition of a portfolio?

A group of programs to achieve a
specific strategic business goal

What is a product life cycle?

The cycle of a product's life from
conception to withdrawal

What is a project life cycle?

What you need to do to COMPLETE the work

It varies by industry and type of project

What is the project management process?

What you need to do to MANAGE the work

Initiating

Planning

Executing

Monitoring and controlling

Closing

What is a project management office?

A department that centralizes the management of projects

Provides the policies, methodologies, and templates for managing projects within the organization

or

Provides support, guidance, and training to others in the organization on how to manage projects

or

Provides project managers for different projects, and is responsible for the results of those projects

What are project constraints?

Cost

Time

Scope

Quality

Risk

Resources

Customer satisfaction

Constraints are used to help evaluate
competing demands

Who are stakeholders?

Anyone whose interests may be positively or negatively impacted by the project, including:

Project manager

Customer

Sponsor

Performing organization

Team

Funding sources

End user

Society

PMO

What should we do with stakeholders?

Identify all of them

Determine all of their requirements

Determine all of their expectations

Communicate with them

Manage their influence

What are three primary forms of organization?

PM Framework

Functional

Projectized

Matrix

What is a functional organization?

The company is grouped by areas
of specialization (e.g., accounting,
marketing)

What is a projectized organization?

The company is grouped by project

The team has no department to go to at project end

The project manager has total control of the resources

What is a matrix organization?

A blend of functional and projectized
organization where the team members
have two bosses (the project manager
and functional manager)

What is a strong matrix organization?

A matrix organization where the balance
of power rests with the project manager
instead of the functional manager

What is a weak matrix organization?

A matrix organization where the balance of power rests with the functional manager instead of the project manager

The project manager's role may include:

Project expediter

Project coordinator

What is a balanced matrix organization?

A matrix organization where power is equally balanced between the project manager and the functional manager

This is the preferred form of matrix

What occurs during the initiating
process group?

Formal authorization of a project or phase

Project manager is provided with information necessary to begin the project

What occurs during the planning
process group?

It is determined:

Whether the project objectives, as stated in the project charter, can be achieved

How the project will be accomplished

What occurs during the executing
process group?

Work defined in the project management plan is completed to meet project objectives

What occurs during the monitoring and controlling process group?

Project performance is measured to the project management plan

Variances are determined and addressed

What occurs during the closing process group?

Acceptance of the final product of the project is obtained and documented

Lessons learned are completed

Files are indexed and archived

Which process group must be completed
in a certain order?

Planning is the only process group with a set order

What does "input" mean?

"What do I need before I can...."

What does "output" mean?

"What will I have when I am done with...."

What is the process of integration management?

Develop Project Charter

Develop Project Management Plan

Direct and Manage Project Execution

Monitor and Control Project Work

Perform Integrated Change Control

Close Project or Phase

What are the methods to select a
project?

Benefit measurement (comparative)

Constrained optimization
(mathematical)

What is the Develop Project
Management Plan process?

What is its output?

The process of creating a project management plan that is bought into, approved, realistic, and formal

Output: The project management plan

What is included in a project
management plan?

Project management processes for the project

Management plans for knowledge areas

Scope, schedule, and cost baselines

Requirements management plan

Change management plan

Configuration management plan

Process improvement plan

What are project documents?

Any documents used to manage a
project that are not part of the project
management plan

They include:
Project charter
Statement of work
Contracts
Stakeholder register
Requirements documentation
Activity list
Quality metrics
Risk register
Issue log
Change log
and any other such documentation

What are key outputs of the Direct and
Manage Project Execution process?

Deliverables

Work performance information

Change requests

Updates to the project management plan and project documents

What are key outputs of the Monitor and Control Project Work process?

Change requests

Updates to the project management plan and project documents

What are key outputs of the Perform Integrated Change Control process?

Change request status updates

Updates to the project management plan
and project documents

What are key outputs of the Close
Project or Phase process?

Final product

Formal acceptance

Organizational process assets updates

Explain the project manager's role as an integrator.

Making sure all the pieces of the project
are properly coordinated and put
together into one cohesive whole

What is a project charter?

How does it help the project?

A document issued by the sponsor during project initiating that:

Formally recognizes the existence of the project

Gives the project manager authority

Documents the business need, justificaton, customer requirements and the product or service to satisfy those requirements

What is a business case?

The project purpose and justification

What is a kickoff meeting?

When does it occur?

A meeting of all parties to the project (project stakeholders, including sellers) to make sure everyone is "on the same page"

It is held at the end of the planning process group

What are baselines?

Parts of the project management plan used to measure performance against

Schedule baseline

Scope baseline

Cost baseline

These baselines are combined to create the performance measurement baseline

Baselines can change with approved changes

What is the project statement of work?

Describes need, product scope, and how the project fits into the strategic plan

Created by the customer/sponsor prior to the beginning of the project

Later refined in the project scope statement

What is a work authorization system?

The project manager's system for authorizing the start of work packages or activities

It ensures work is done at the right time and in the proper sequence

What is a configuration management
plan?

A plan to make sure everyone knows what version of the scope, schedule, and other components of the project management plan are the latest versions

It defines how you will manage changes to the deliverables and the resulting documentation

What is a change management plan?

A system of formal procedures, set up in advance, defining how project deliverables and documentation are controlled, changed, and approved

What are enterprise environmental factors?

When are they used?

Company culture and existing systems the project will have to deal with or can make use of

They are used throughout the project management process

What are organizational process assets?

When are they used?

Company processes and procedures

Historical information

Lessons learned

They are used throughout the project management process

What is historical information?

Records of past projects, including lessons learned, used to plan and manage future projects

Records of the current project which will become part of organizational process assets

What is a project management
information system?

The manual and automated system to submit and track changes and monitor and control project activities

What is a change control board?

Who may be on it?

A group of people that approves or rejects changes

May include:

Project manager

Customer

Experts

Sponsor

Others

For the exam, assume that all projects have change control boards

What are change requests?

When are they approved?

Formal requests to change parts of the project after the project management plan is approved

They are approved in the Perform Integrated Change Control process

What are preventive actions?

Actions taken to deal with anticipated
or possible deviations from the
performance measurement baseline

What are corrective actions?

Actions taken to bring expected future
project performance in line with the
project management plan

Define present value.

The value today of future cash flows

Define net present value.

The value in today's dollars of some future costs and expenses

For cost, the lower the number the better

For revenue, the higher the number the better

Define internal rate of return.

The rate an investment in the project will return

The higher the number the better

The rate at which a project's inflows and outflows are equal

Define payback period.

The number of time periods to recover the investment

The lower the number the better

Define benefit cost ratio.

$$\frac{\text{Benefit}}{\text{Cost}}$$

The higher the number the better

Define opportunity cost.

The opportunity given up by selecting
one project over another

What are sunk costs?

Expended costs

Define the law of diminishing returns.

The more you put into the effort, the less
you get out of it

Define working capital.

Current assets minus current liabilities

The amount of funds available to spend on projects

What are the two types of depreciation?

Straight Line Depreciation: Depreciate the same amount each time period

Accelerated Depreciation: Depreciate an amount greater than straight line each time period

What is the process of scope management?

Collect Requirements

Define Scope

Create WBS

Verify Scope

Control Scope

What is the definition of scope
management?

Doing all the work, and only the work, included in the project

Determining if work is included in the project or not

In which process is the scope
management plan created?

The scope management plan is created in the integration management process, as part of Develop Project Management Plan

What are key outputs of the Collect Requirements process?

Requirements documentation

Requirements management plan

Requirements traceability matrix

What is a key output of the Define Scope process?

Project scope statement

What are key outputs of the Create WBS process?

Work breakdown structure (WBS)

WBS dictionary

Scope baseline

What are key outputs of the Verify Scope process?

Accepted deliverables

Change requests

Project document updates

What are key outputs of the Control
Scope process?

Work performance measurements

Change requests

Updates to the project management plan
and project documents

Name several requirements gathering techniques.

Interviewing

Focus groups

Facilitated workshops

Brainstorming

Affinity diagrams

Questionnaires

Prototypes

What is included in a requirements traceability matrix?

Requirement identification number

Source of the requirement

Who is assigned to manage the requirement

Status of the requirement

What is a project scope statement?

What are the key items included?

A written description of the project deliverables and the work required to create those deliverables

It includes:

Product scope

Project Scope

Deliverables

Product acceptance criteria

What is not part of the project

Constraints and assumptions

Product analysis is part of which scope management process?

Product analysis occurs during the
Define Scope process

When is a work breakdown structure
(WBS) created, and what is it used for?

Created during project planning by the team and used to define or decompose the project into smaller, more manageable pieces

Used to help determine project staffing, estimating, scheduling, and risk management

What does a work breakdown structure show?

Hierarchy

Interrelationships

Work packages

Control account

Numbering system

What is decomposition?

Subdividing the major deliverables into
smaller, more manageable components

What is a WBS dictionary?

A description of the work to be done for
each work package

How are work packages different from activities?

Activities are generated from each work package

Work packages are shown in a WBS

Activities are shown in an activity list and network diagram

What is the Verify Scope process?

When is it done?

The process of formalizing acceptance of the project scope by the stakeholders/customer

It is done during project monitoring and controlling and at the end of each phase of the project life cycle

What is the difference between product scope and project scope?

Product scope is requirements that relate to the product of the project

Project scope is the project work needed to accomplish the product scope

What makes up the scope baseline?

Project scope statement

WBS

WBS dictionary

What is the process of time management?

Define Activities

Sequence Activities

Estimate Activity Resources

Estimate Activity Durations

Develop Schedule

Control Schedule

In which process is the schedule management plan created?

The schedule management plan is created in integration management, as part of the Develop Project Management Plan process.

What are key outputs of the Define
Activities process?

Activity list

Activity attributes

Milestone list

What are key outputs of the Sequence
Activities process?

Network diagrams

Project document updates

What are key outputs of the Estimate
Activity Resources process?

Activity resource requirements

Resource breakdown structure

What are key outputs of the Estimate
Activity Durations process?

Activity duration estimates

Project document updates

What is the Develop Schedule process?

What are its key outputs?

The actions and tools necessary to create a bought into, approved, realistic, and formal project schedule

Outputs:

 Project schedule

 Schedule baseline

What are key outputs of the Control
Schedule process?

Work performance measurements

Change requests

What are mandatory dependencies and discretionary dependencies?

Mandatory: One activity MUST be done after or before another; may also be called hard logic

Discretionary: When you PREFER activities to be accomplished in a certain order; may also be called preferred, preferential, or soft logic

What are external dependencies?

Dependencies based on the needs of a
party OUTSIDE the project

What is a resource breakdown structure?

An organizational chart or table showing
identified resources by category

What is the critical path?

How does it help the project?

The longest path through the network diagram

It shows the project manager the shortest time in which the project can be completed

It shows the project manager where to focus his or her time

It is used in compressing or adjusting the schedule

What is the near-critical path?

The path closest in length to the critical
path

Define lag.

Waiting time inserted into the schedule

Define total float and the formula for total float.

The amount of time an activity can be delayed without delaying the project

Formula:

Late start – Early start

OR

Late finish – Early finish

Define free float and project float.

Free Float: The amount of time an activity can be delayed without delaying the early start date of its successor

Project Float: The amount of time the project can be delayed without affecting the project's required end date; the desired project end date minus the actual end date

What are the methods to compress a
schedule?

Crashing

Fast tracking

What is crashing?

Schedule compression through analyzing cost and schedule trade-offs to obtain the greatest compression for the least cost while maintaining scope

What is fast tracking?

Schedule compression by doing more
critical path activities in parallel

What is the critical chain method?

A schedule network analysis tool that
makes use of buffers

What is reestimating?

Estimating the project again after
planning to make sure you can still meet
the end date, budget, or other objectives

What is resource leveling?

Keeping the amount of resources used for each time period constant, thus affecting the project duration

What is the schedule baseline?

The approved schedule with any approved changes, used to measure project schedule performance

What are the main tools for displaying a schedule?

Network diagrams

Bar charts

Milestone charts

What do network diagrams show?

Interdependencies between activities

How project activities will flow from beginning to end

Network diagrams may also be used to determine the critical path

What do simple bar charts show?

Project schedule or project status

What do milestone charts show?

High-level project status

What is Monte Carlo analysis?

A schedule network analysis technique

It is used to simulate the project to determine how likely you are to get the project completed by any specific date or for any specific cost

It is also used in the Perform Quantitative Risk Analysis process to determine an overall level of risk on the project

What are the following rules?

50/50 rule

20/80 rule

0/100 rule

Methods of progress reporting

50 percent (or 20 percent or 0 percent) of the effort is reported complete when an activity begins

The balance (50 percent, 80 percent, or 100 percent) is recorded only when an activity is finished

What is the process of cost management?

Estimate Costs

Determine Budget

Control Costs

In which process is the cost management plan created?

The cost management plan is created
in integration management as part of
the Develop Project Management Plan
process

What are key outputs of the Estimate
Costs process?

Activity cost estimates

Updates to the project management plan
and project documents

What are key outputs of the Determine
Budget process?

Cost baseline

Funding requirements

What are key outputs of the Control
Costs process?

Work performance measurements

Budget forecasts

Change requests

Updates to the project management plan
and project documents

Name inputs to the Estimate Costs
process.

Scope baseline

Project schedule

Human resource plan

Enterprise environmental factors

Organizational process assets

Risk register

What are the main approaches to cost or schedule estimating?

Analogous estimating

Bottom-up estimating

Parametric estimating

Three-point estimates

One-time estimates

What is analogous estimating?

Top-down estimating that uses expert judgement and looks at the past to predict the future

"The last three projects cost $25,000, or took six months, and so should this one"

What is bottom-up estimating?

Creating estimates based on the details of the project (e.g., from the bottom of the work breakdown structure), which are then rolled up into project estimates

What is parametric estimating?

Calculating estimates using historical
information (e.g., cost per line of code,
hours per installation)

What is earned value measurement?

A method of measuring project performance that looks at the value earned for work accomplished

It can be used to predict future cost performance and project completion dates

What is the range for a rough order of magnitude estimate?

+/-50 percent from actual

What is the range for a budget estimate?

-10 percent to +25 percent from actual

What is the range for a definitive
estimate?

+/-10 percent from actual

What is the difference between a cost budget and a cost baseline?

The cost budget adds management
reserve to the cost baseline

What is the formula for cost variance?

$$EV - AC = CV$$

What is the formula for schedule variance?

Cost Management

$$EV - PV = SV$$

What is the formula for cost
performance index?

Cost Management

$$EV / AC = CPI$$

What is the formula for schedule
performance index?

$$EV / PV = SPI$$

What are the formulas for estimate at
completion?

$$AC + \text{Bottom-up ETC} = EAC$$

$$BAC / CPI^c = EAC$$

$$AC + (BAC - EV) = EAC$$

$$AC + \frac{(BAC - EV)}{(CPI^c \times SPI^c)} = EAC$$

What is the formula for estimate to complete?

$$EAC - AC = ETC$$

What is the formula for variance at completion?

$$BAC - EAC = VAC$$

What is the formula for TCPI?

Cost Management

$$\frac{(BAC - EV)}{(BAC - AC)}$$

Describe a variable cost and a fixed cost chargeable to the project.

Variable Cost: A cost that varies with the amount of work done on the project

Fixed Cost: A cost that does not vary with the amount of work done on the project

Describe a direct cost and an indirect cost chargeable to the project.

Direct Cost: A cost directly attributable to the project

Indirect Cost: Overhead costs

What does life cycle costing mean?

Considering the future cost of operating and maintaining the project or deliverable over its life when planning and managing the project

What is value analysis?

Finding a less costly way of doing
essentially the same work

What is the process of quality management?

Quality Management

Plan Quality

Perform Quality Assurance

Perform Quality Control

What are key outputs of the Plan Quality process?

Quality management plan

Quality metrics

Quality checklists

Process improvement plan

Project document updates

What are key outputs of the Perform
Quality Assurance process?

Change requests

Updates to the project management plan and project documents

Organizational process assets updates

What are key outputs of the Perform
Quality Control process?

Quality control measurements

Validated changes

Validated deliverables

Change requests

Updates to the project management plan
and project documents

What is the definition of quality?

The degree to which the project fulfills requirements

What does gold plating mean?

Adding extra items and services that do not necessarily contribute added value or quality to customer deliverables

What is marginal analysis?

An analysis to determine when optimal quality is reached

An analysis to determine the point where incremental revenue from improvement equals the incremental cost to secure it

What is a process improvement plan?

A plan for analyzing processes used
on the project to decrease defects, save
time and money, and increase customer
satisfaction

What are quality metrics?

Specific measures of quality to be used on the project in the Perform Quality Assurance and Perform Quality Control processes

What does continuous improvement
mean?

The ongoing enhancement of a product or service through small, continuous improvements in quality

How much inventory is maintained in a just in time environment?

How does this affect attention to quality?

Little inventory is maintained

It forces attention to quality

What does ISO 9000 stand for?

One of the International Organization for Standardization (ISO) international quality standards that asks, "Do you have a quality standard, and are you following it?"

What is the definition of total quality management, or TQM?

A comprehensive management philosophy that encourages finding ways to continuously improve the quality of business practices, products, or services

What does the phrase "prevention over inspection" mean?

The cost of avoiding or preventing
mistakes is much less than the cost of
correcting them

What does mutually exclusive mean?

Two events that cannot occur in a single trial

For example, you can't get a 5 and a 6 on a single roll of a die

What does statistical independence
mean?

The probability of event "B" occurring does not depend on event "A" occurring

For example, the outcome of a second roll of a die is not influenced by (dependent on) the outcome of the first roll

What is a normal distribution curve?

A symmetric bell-shaped frequency distribution curve

The most common probability distribution

What do 3 sigma and 6 sigma refer to?

These are often used as quality standards

3 Sigma: +/- 3 standard deviations from the distribution mean under which 99.73% of all items are acceptable

6 Sigma: +/- 6 standard deviations from the mean under which 99.99985% of all items are acceptable

6 sigma is a higher quality standard than 3 sigma

What is the difference between a
population and a sample?

Population: The total number of individual members, items, or elements comprising a uniquely defined group (e.g., all women)

Sample: A subset of population members (e.g., women over the age of 30 in England)

Who has responsibility for quality on a project?

The project manager is ultimately responsible, but the team members must inspect their own work

What are the impacts of poor quality?

Increased costs

Low morale

Low customer satisfaction

Increased risk

Rework

Schedule delays

What are examples of costs
of conformance and costs of
nonconformance?

Which costs should be greater?

What are costs of nonconformance
associated with?

Costs of conformance:

- Quality training
- Studies
- Surveys

Costs of nonconformance:

- Rework
- Scrap
- Inventory costs
- Warranty costs

The costs of conformance should be less than the costs of nonconformance

Costs of nonconformance are associated with poor quality

Name key tools and techniques used in
the Plan Quality process.

Cost-benefit analysis

Cost of quality

Control charts

Benchmarking

Design of experiments

Statistical sampling

Flowcharting

Define benchmarking.

Comparing your project to other
projects to get ideas for improvement
and to measure quality performance

Define cost-benefit analysis.

Comparing the costs of an effort to the
benefits of that effort

What is design of experiments?

A statistical method for changing important variables to determine what combination will improve overall quality

What are some of the tools and techniques used in the Perform Quality Assurance process?

Process analysis

Quality audits

Plan Quality and Perform Quality Control tools and techniques

What are quality audits?

Structured reviews of quality activities

These audits often result in lessons learned for the organization

Name the seven basic tools of quality.

Cause and effect diagram

Control chart

Flowcharting

Histogram

Pareto chart

Run chart

Scatter diagram

What is defect repair?

Rework required when a component of
the project does not meet specifications

What is a cause and effect diagram?

An illustration that helps determine the possible causes of a problem

It is also called a fishbone or Ishikawa diagram

What is a quality checklist?

A list of items to inspect, a list of steps to perform, or a picture of an item with space to note any defects found during inspection

What is a Pareto chart?

A histogram that arranges the results from most frequent to least frequent to help identify which root causes are resulting in the most problems

What is the 80/20 principle?

80 percent of problems are caused by 20 percent of the root causes

What is statistical sampling?

Inspecting by choosing only part of a
population (a sample) to test

What is a control chart?

A specialized trend chart documenting whether a measured process is in or out of statistical control

What are control limits?

The acceptable range of variation on a
control chart

What are the specification limits on a control chart?

The customer's definition of acceptable product/service characteristics and tolerances

What does out of control mean?

There is a lack of consistency and predictability in the process, due to the existence of assignable causes

What does the rule of seven mean?

Seven consecutive data points appearing on a control chart on one side of the mean, suggesting that the process is out of statistical control

What is a special cause variation?

A data point on a control chart or rule of seven indicating that the measured process is out of statistical control and that the cause(s) of the event must be investigated

What is the process of human resource management?

Develop Human Resource Plan

Acquire Project Team

Develop Project Team

Manage Project Team

What is the key output of the Develop
Human Resource Plan process?

Human resource plan

What are key outputs of the Acquire
Project Team process?

Project staff assignments

Resource calendars

Project management plan updates

What is a key output of the Develop
Project Team process?

Team performance assessments (Think of this as evaluating team effectiveness)

What is a key output of the Manage
Project Team process?

Change requests

Describe the roles and responsibilities of
all the people involved in a project.

This topic cannot be summarized here, but it is critical to understand who does what

See the roles and responsibilities section in the Human Resource Management chapters of the *PMP® Exam Prep* and *CAPM® Exam Prep* books for more on this topic

What are key responsibilities of the
sponsor on a project?

Provide information regarding the initial scope of the project

Issue the charter

Provide funding

May dictate dates

Approve the final project management plan

Approve or reject changes or authorize a change control board

Be involved in risk management

Describe key responsibilities of the team
on a project.

Identify requirements, constraints, and assumptions

Create the work breakdown structure and help with project planning

Estimate activities

Participate in risk management

Complete activities

Comply with quality and communications plans

Recommend changes to the project

Describe key responsibilities of the stakeholders on a project.

They may help:

Identify requirements and constraints

Plan the project

Approve changes

Perform the risk management process

Describe key responsibilities of
functional managers on a project.

Participate in planning

Approve the final project management plan

Approve the final schedule

Assist with problems related to team member performance

Manage activities that happen within their functional area

What are the key elements of a human resource plan?

When and how human resource requirements will be met

Roles and responsibilities

Project organization charts

Staffing management plan:

Staff acquisition plan

Resource calendars

Staff release plan

Staff training needs

Recognition and rewards

Compliance

Safety

What are some key activities involved in developing the project team?

Hold team-building activities throughout the project

Obtain and provide training where needed

Establish ground rules

Create and give recognition and rewards

Place team members in the same location (co-location)

What are some key activities involved in managing a project team?

Use negotiation and leadership skills

Observe what is happening

Use an issue log

Keep in touch

Complete project performance appraisals

Actively look for and help resolve conflicts that the team cannot resolve on their own

What is a team performance assessment?

An assessment by the project manager of
project team effectiveness

Name different types of power.

Formal

Reward

Penalty

Expert

Referent

Name some leadership and management styles a project manager may choose to use.

Directing

Facilitating

Coaching

Supporting

Autocratic

Consultative

Consultative –
Autocratic

Consensus

Delegating

Bureaucratic

Charismatic

Democratic

Laissez-faire

Analytical

Driver

Influencing

Name the most common sources of conflict on projects.

Schedules

Priorities

Resources

Technical opinions

Administrative procedures

Cost

Personality (least frequent source)

Name conflict resolution techniques.

Confronting (problem solving)

Compromising

Withdrawal (avoidance)

Smoothing (accommodating)

Collaborating

Forcing

Define confronting (problem solving).

Define compromising.

Define collaborating.

Confronting (problem solving): Solving the real problem (win-win)

Compromising: Making all parties somewhat happy (lose-lose)

Collaborating: Trying to incorporate multiple viewpoints to achieve consensus

Define withdrawal (avoidance).

Define smoothing (accommodating).

Define forcing.

Withdrawal (avoidance): Postponing a project decision or avoiding addressing the problem

Smoothing (accommodating): Emphasizing agreement rather than differences of opinion

Forcing: Pushing one viewpoint at the expense of another; e.g., "Do it my way"

What are some of the project manager's human resource responsibilities?

Determine needed resources

Negotiate for optimal available resources

Create a team directory

Create project-related job descriptions for team members

Make sure roles and responsibilities are clear

Ensure that team members obtain needed training

Create recognition and rewards systems

Create a human resource plan

What is a project performance appraisal?

An evaluation of individual team
member effectiveness

What is an issue log?

A record of project issues, persons
responsible for resolving issues, issue
status, and target resolution dates

What is Maslow's theory?

Maslow's hierarchy of needs: People are motivated according to the following hierarchy of needs:

Self-actualization (highest motivation)

Esteem

Social

Safety

Physiological

What theories did McGregor describe?

Theory X: Managers who accept this theory believe that people need to be constantly watched

Theory Y: Managers who accept this theory believe that people want to achieve and can work without supervision

What did Herzberg's theory describe?

Hygiene factors (e.g., working conditions, salary, personal life, etc.)

Motivating agents (e.g., responsibility, self-actualization, professional growth, etc.)

What is McClelland's theory of needs?

People are motivated by one of three needs:

Need for achievement

Need for affiliation

Need for power

What are the stages of team formation and development?

Forming

Storming

Norming

Performing

Adjourning

Why is releasing resources the last
activity in closure?

The team and other resources are needed
to help complete closure

What is the "halo effect"?

A tendency to rate team members high or low on all factors because of a high or low rating on a specific factor (e.g., A team member will be a great project manager because she always completes her activities on time)

What is the process of communications management?

Identify Stakeholders

Plan Communications

Distribute Information

Report Performance

Manage Stakeholder Expectations

What are key outputs of the Identify
Stakeholders process?

Stakeholder register

Stakeholder management strategy

What is the key output of the Plan
Communications process?

Communications management plan

What are key outputs of the Distribute
Information process?

Organizational process assets updates
(this includes records of all the
information communicated during this
process)

What are key outputs of the Manage
Stakeholder Expectations process?

Updates to the project management plan
and project documents

Change requests

Organizational process assets updates

What are key outputs of the Report
Performance process?

Performance reports

Change requests

What information regarding stakeholders is documented in a stakeholder register?

Name

Contact information

Requirements and expectations

Impact and influence

Describe the communications model
and its components.

Messages are encoded, transmitted, received, and decoded, and must include attention to:

Nonverbal communication

Paralingual communication

Effective listening (including using active listening and giving feedback)

Noise

How much of communication is nonverbal?

About 55 percent

What does paralingual mean?

Pitch and tone of voice

Name communication types.

Formal

Informal

Written

Verbal

Define interactive, push, and pull communications.

Interactive: The sender provides information and recipients receive and respond to that information

Push: The sender provides information but does not expect feedback on that information

Pull: The sender places information in a central location and recipients are responsible for retrieving that information

How much time do project managers spend communicating?

90 percent

What is communication technology?

Face-to-face interactions

Telephone

Fax

E-mail

The project manager must determine the appropriate technology to use in each situation

Name communication blockers.

Noise

Distance

Improper encoding

Negative statements

Hostility

Language

Culture

Describe the rules for effective meetings.

Set a time limit

Schedule in advance

Create an agenda with team input

Distribute agenda in advance

Lead meeting with a set of rules

See the Communications Chapter in *PMP® Exam Prep* for more on this topic

What is the formula for communication channels?

$$[N (N-1)] / 2$$

What are lessons learned?

What do we do with them?

What went right, what went wrong, and what could be done differently

Used in planning a project

Generated by the project to be used by other projects in the future

What is the process of risk management?

Plan Risk Management

Identify Risks

Perform Qualitative Risk Analysis

Perform Quantitative Risk Analysis

Plan Risk Responses

Monitor and Control Risks

What is a key output of the Plan Risk
Management process?

Risk management plan

What is a key output of the Identify
Risks process?

Risk Management

Risk register

What key outputs of the Perform Qualitative Risk Analysis process are added to the risk register?

Risk ranking for the project

Prioritized risks and their probability
and impact ratings

Risks grouped by category

List of risks requiring additional analysis
and response

Watchlist

What key outputs of the Perform Quantitative Risk Analysis process are added to the risk register?

Prioritized list of quantified risks

Possible realistic and achievable
completion dates and project costs

Quantified probability of meeting
project objectives

What are key outputs of the Plan Risk
Responses process?

Risk register updates:

  Residual risks

  Contingency plans

  Risk response owners

  Secondary risks

  Triggers

  Fallback plans

  Reserves for time and cost

Updates to the project management plan
and project documents

What are key outputs of the Monitor and
Control Risks process?

Risk register updates:

Outcomes of risk reassessments and risk audits

Updates to the risk register

Closing of risks that are no longer applicable

Details of what happened when risks occurred

Lessons learned

Change requests

Updates to the project management plan and project documents

Risk Management

What is a risk?

An occurrence that can affect a project
for better (opportunity) or worse (threat)

Describe key things one needs to determine about each risk.

Probability

Impact

Timing

Frequency

Someone who is risk averse is:

Unwilling to take risks

What is risk tolerance?

The areas of risk acceptable

Name the inputs to the risk management process.

Project background information

Historical records from previous projects

Organizational process assets

Project charter

Project scope statement

Team

WBS

Network diagram

Staffing management plan

Procurement management plan

What are risk categories?

Lists of common sources of risk, including:

Technical

Project management

Schedule

Cost

Quality

Scope

Resources

Customer satisfaction

Others

What are risk identification techniques?

Documentation reviews

Brainstorming

Delphi technique

Root cause analysis

Interviewing

SWOT

Checklist analysis

Assumptions analysis

Diagramming techniques

What are the types of risks?

Risk Management

Business

Pure

What are risk triggers?

Early warning signs that a risk event has occurred or is about to occur

What is assumptions analysis?

When is it done?

Exploring the validity of project assumptions

It is done during the Identify Risks process

What is risk data quality assessment?

When is it done?

Determining how well understood is the risk information

A method to test reliability of risk information collected

It is done during the Perform Qualitative Risk Analysis process

What is a probability and impact matrix?

The company's scale used to determine which risks continue through the risk management process

What is the formula for expected
monetary value?

Probability times impact

What is a decision tree?

A model of a decision to be made which includes the probabilities and impacts of future events

Who is a risk response owner?

The person assigned to execute risk
responses for each critical risk

Name and define the risk response
strategies for threats.

Avoid: Eliminate a specific threat by eliminating the cause

Mitigate: Reduce the probability or impact of a threat

Accept:

Passive acceptance—do nothing; if it happens, it happens

Active acceptance—develop contingency plans

Transfer: Make another party responsible for a risk; may include outsourcing, insurance, warranties, bonds, and guarantees

Name and define the risk response
strategies for opportunities.

Exploit: Make sure the opportunity occurs

Share: Allocate ownership to a third party

Enhance: Increase probability or impacts

Accept:

Passive acceptance—Do nothing; if it happens, it happens

Active acceptance—Develop contingency plans

What are residual risks?

Risks that remain after risk response planning:

Risks for which contingency and fallback plans have been created

Risks which have been accepted

What are secondary risks?

New risks created by the implementation
of risk response strategies

How does buying insurance relate to risk response planning?

It exchanges an unknown risk for a known risk

It is a method to decrease project risk

How does a contract relate to risk response planning?

A contract helps allocate and mitigate risks

A risk analysis is done before a contract is signed

What are contingency plans?

Planned responses to risks

What are fallback plans?

Actions that will be taken if the
contingency plan is not effective

What does a revised project management plan have to do with risk management?

The components of the project management plan will need to be updated based on the results of risk planning

What are reserves?

Time or cost added to the project to account for risk

There are two types of reserves:

Management reserve

Contingency reserve

What is a contingency reserve?

Time or cost allocated to cover known unknowns

It is included in the cost baseline

What is a management reserve?

Time or cost allocated to cover unknown unknowns

It is included in the cost budget

What are risk reassessments?

When do they occur?

Reviews of the risk management plan and risk register

They occur during the Monitor and Control Risks process

What is reserve analysis?

When is it done?

Managing the reserves and making sure the amount remaining is adequate

It is done during the Monitor and Control Risks, Estimate Activity Durations, and Determine Budget processes

What are risk audits?

Examining and documenting the
effectiveness of the risk process and the
risk response owners

What is the process of procurement management?

Plan Procurements

Conduct Procurements

Administer Procurements

Close Procurements

Name inputs to the procurement
management process.

Enterprise environmental factors

Organizational process assets

Scope baseline

Risk register

Project schedule

Initial cost estimates for contracted work

Cost baseline for the project

What are key outputs of the Plan
Contracting process?

Procurement management plan

Procurement statement of work

Make-or-buy decisions

Procurement documents

What are key outputs of the Conduct
Procurements process?

Selected sellers

Procurement contract

What are key outputs of the Administer
Procurements process?

Procurement documentation

Change requests

Project management plan updates

What are key outputs of the Close
Procurements process?

Closed procurements

Formal acceptance

What is a procurement management plan?

A plan for how each contract
procurement will be administered

What is the difference between centralized and decentralized contracting?

Centralized contracting: There is one procurement, and the procurement manager handles procurements on many projects

Decentralized contracting: A procurement manager is assigned to one project full-time and reports directly to the project manager

What is required for a legal contract?

Offer

Acceptance

Consideration

Legal capacity

Legal purpose

What is a contract?

It may include all of the following:

Legal terms

Business terms

Procurement statement of work

Marketing literature

Drawings

Describe the project manager's role in procurement.

Understand the procurement process

Make sure the work described in the contract is complete

Be involved in the whole procurement process

Help tailor the contract to the project

Incorporate mitigation and allocation of risks into the contract

Name the advantages of centralized contracting.

Increased expertise in contracting

Standardized practices

Clear career path

Name the disadvantages of centralized contracting.

One person works on many projects

It may be difficult to obtain contracting help when needed

Name the advantages of decentralized contracting.

Easier access to contracting expertise

More loyalty to the project

Name the disadvantages of decentralized
contracting.

No home for the contracts person after the project

Less focus on improving contracting expertise

Inefficient use of resources

Little standardization of contracting processes from one project to the next

What is a make-or-buy decision?

Analysis of whether the performing organization should do the work or buy the services/supplies from outside the organization

What are the main types of contracts?

Cost reimbursable

Fixed price

Time and material

Purchase order

What is a cost reimbursable contract?

All costs are reimbursed

What is a cost plus fixed fee contract?

All costs are reimbursed

The fee is fixed at a certain monetary
amount

What is a cost plus percentage of cost contract?

All costs are reimbursed, plus a specific percentage of costs as fee or profit

What is a cost plus incentive fee contract?

Costs are reimbursed plus an incentive, usually an additional fee, for exceeding performance criteria that have been determined in advance

What is a time and material contract?

Usually a fixed hourly rate or a fixed cost
per item, plus a reimbursable component
for expenses or materials

What is a fixed price contract?

There is only one fee for accomplishing
all the work

What is a fixed price incentive fee contract?

Total price is fixed, but an additional amount may be paid for exceeding performance criteria determined in advance

What is a fixed price economic price adjustment contract?

A fixed price contract with an allowable adjustment for price increase, due to cost increases in later time periods

Describe how contract administration
efforts will be different with each
contract form.

This critical concept cannot be summarized here.

See the Procurement Chapter in *CAPM® Exam Prep* or *PMP® Exam Prep* for more on this topic

What is a purchase order?

A unilateral contract

What are incentives?

What might they be used for?

Help bring the seller's objectives in line with the buyer's

Incentives for:

Time

Cost

Quality

Scope

Who has the cost risk in a cost reimbursable contract?

In a fixed price contract?

Risk in a cost reimbursable contract is borne by the buyer

Risk in a fixed price contract is borne by the seller

Name the types of procurement
statements of work.

Performance

Functional

Design

What are procurement documents?

Request for proposal (RFP)

Invitation for bid (IFB)

Request for quotation (RFQ)

What are standard contract terms and conditions?

What are special provisions?

Standard contract terms and provisions: Terms and conditions which are used for all contracts within the company

Special provisions: Terms and conditions created for the unique needs of the project

Created with the input of the project manager

Name common terms and conditions
that may be in a contract.

Please review the long list of terms and conditions and what they mean in the Procurement Management chapter of *CAPM® Exam Prep* or *PMP® Exam Prep*

What is a letter of intent?

A letter from the buyer, without legal binding, saying the buyer intends to hire the seller

What does privity refer to?

Contractual relationships between two
or more companies

What does non-competitive
procurement mean?

Work awarded to a single source or sole source without competition

When are evaluation criteria created and used?

What do they refer to?

Rationale that the buyer will use to weight or score sellers' proposals

Created during the Plan Procurements process

Used during the Conduct Procurements process to pick a seller

What is a bidder conference?

What should be watched out for?

A meeting with prospective sellers to make sure all understand the procurement and have a chance to ask questions

Watch for:

Collusion

Sellers not asking questions

All questions and answers are distributed to all

What is a qualified seller list?

A list of sellers who have been pre-approved

What are objectives of negotiation?

Obtain a fair and reasonable price

Develop a good relationship with the
other side

Name some negotiation tactics.

Attacks

Good guy/Bad guy

Deadline

Lying

Missing man

Delay

Withdrawal

Fait accompli

Name some of the project manager's activities during the Administer Procurements process.

Review invoices

Integrated change control

Interpret the contract

Monitor performance against the contract

Risk management

Please see the long list in the Procurement Management chapter of *CAPM® Exam Prep* or *PMP® Exam Prep*

Why might there be conflict between the contract administrator and the project manager?

The contract administrator is the only one with the power to change the contract (including the project scope)

What is a contract change control
system?

A system created to modify the contract
and to control changes to the contract

What must be done for all contract changes?

They must be formally documented

What is the purpose of a procurement performance review?

To identify seller's successes or failures, and allow the buyer to rate the seller's ability to perform

Define claims administration.

Managing contested changes and
constructive changes (claims) requested
by the seller

What is the key function of a records management system?

Maintain an index of contract documentation and records to assist in retrieval

Part of the project management information system

Name the guidelines for interpreting
what is or is not included in the contract.

Please see the Contract Interpretation discussion and exercise in the Procurement Management chapter of *PMP® Exam Prep* for more on this topic. The CAPM exam does not focus on contract interpretation.

What occurs during the Close
Procurements process?

Product verification

Procurement audit

Financial closure

What is a procurement audit?

A structured review of the procurement process and determination of lessons learned to help other procurements

What does professional and social
responsibility entail?

Responsibility

Respect

Fairness

Honesty

For the PMP exam, make sure you read the extensive information on this topic in the Professional and Social Responsibility chapter of *PMP® Exam Prep.* The CAPM Exam does not test on professional and social responsibility.

What does "responsibility" in project management mean?

Make decisions based on the best interests of the company and the team

Do what you say you will do

Acknowledge your errors

Uphold laws, including copyright laws

Report unethical behavior

What does "respect" in project
management mean?

Maintain an attitude of mutual cooperation

Respect cultural differences

Engage in good faith negotiations

Be direct in dealing with conflict

What does "fairness" in project management mean?

Act impartially

Look for and disclose conflicts of interest

Do not discriminate

Honor your duty of loyalty

What does "honesty" in project
management mean?

Try to understand the truth

Be truthful in all communications

Create an environment where others tell the truth

Notes

Notes

Notes

Notes